ANIMALS
That Make a Difference!

Bats

Ashley Lee

Explore other books at:
WWW.ENGAGEBOOKS.COM

VANCOUVER, B.C.

ℯ→ WWW.ENGAGEBOOKS.COM

Bats: Level 1
Animals That Make a Difference!
Lee, Ashley 1995
Text © 2021 Engage Books

Edited by: A.R. Roumanis
and Lauren Dick

Text set in Arial Regular.
Chapter headings set in Arial Black.

FIRST EDITION / FIRST PRINTING

LIBRARY AND ARCHIVES CANADA CATALOGUING IN PUBLICATION

Title: Animals That Make a Difference: Bats Level 1
Names: Lee, Ashley, author.

Identifiers: Canadiana (print) 20200309129 | Canadiana (ebook) 20200309137
ISBN 978-1-77437-672-0 (hardcover)
ISBN 978-1-77437-673-7 (softcover)
ISBN 978-1-77437-674-4 (pdf)
ISBN 978-1-77437-675-1 (epub)
ISBN 978-1-77437-676-8 (kindle)

Subjects:
LCSH: Bats—Juvenile literature
LCSH: Human-animal relationships—Juvenile literature

Classification: LCC QL737.C5 L44 2020 | DDC J599.4—DC23

Contents

What Are Bats?

Bats are the only mammals that can fly.

Mammals are covered in hair and have bones in their back. They feed their babies milk.

What Do Bats Look Like?

The smallest bats are only 6 inches (15 centimeters) wide. The largest bats can be up to 6 feet (1.8 meters) wide.

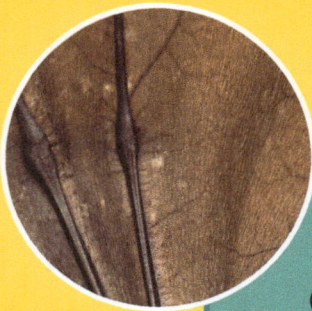

Bat wings are made of thin skin. The skin is stretched between the front and back legs.

A bat's ears are large compared to the size of its head. Bats use their ears to find food and other bats.

Bats have claws on their feet. They use their claws to hold things.

Where Do Bats Live?

Bats make homes called roosts. Roosts are used for sleeping. Most bats make roosts in caves or old buildings.

Most bats live in tropical areas. Tube-nosed bats live in Australia. Indian flying fox bats live in India. Sulawesi fruit bats come from Indonesia.

Arctic Ocean

Indonesia

Europe

Asia

Pacific Ocean

India

Africa

Atlantic Ocean

Australia

Australia

Southern Ocean

Antarctica

Legend
Land
Ocean

N

0   2,000 miles

0   4,000 kilometers

9

What Do Bats Eat?

Most bats eat fruit or insects. Some bats drink a sweet liquid from flowers called nectar. A few bats eat small animals. They eat birds, frogs, and lizards.

Some bats find food by using special cries. These cries bounce back to the bat when they hit an object. Bats hear their cry and can tell where small animals are. This is called echolocation.

How Do Bats Talk to Each Other?

Bats use chirps and cries to talk to each other. They use these sounds to find other bats or warn others of danger.

Some bat sounds are so high-pitched they cannot be heard by people.

Bat Life Cycle

Baby bats are called pups. They learn to fly when they are 3 weeks old.

Pups stay in groups called nurseries. They are cared for by female bats.

Pups are fully grown at 2 months old. This is when they leave the nursery.

Most bats live for 10 to 20 years. Very few bats live more than 30 years.

Curious Facts About Bats

Bats lick themselves to keep clean.

The oldest known living bat was 41 years old.

Bats can eat more than 1,000 insects in an hour.

Some bats sleep through winter. This is called hibernation.

Most bats sleep upside down. They hang from their feet.

Bat knees bend backwards.

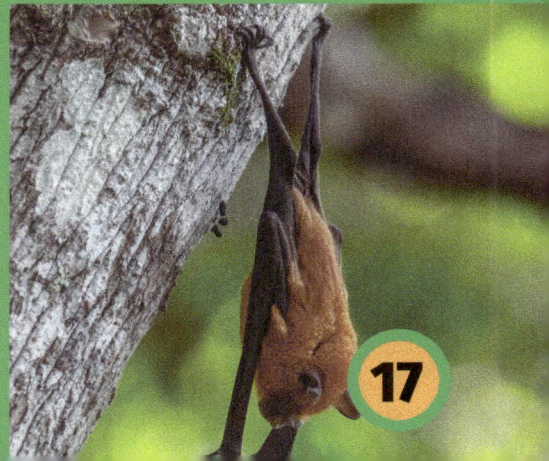

Kinds of Bats

There are more than 1,300 kinds of bats. These are split into two groups. Microbats eat insects. They usually only come out at night.

Megabats eat fruit and nectar. They have larger eyes than microbats. Some megabats come out during the day.

How Bats Help Earth

Bats eat many plant seeds. The seeds come out in their poop. Bat poop helps seeds grow into new plants.

Pollen is a fine powder that flowers make. Female plants need pollen from male plants to make seeds. Bats help spread pollen from one plant to another. This is called pollination.

21

How Bats Help Other Animals

Many animals eat the plants that bats help grow. These animals would have less food to eat without bats.

Desert animals drink water from cacti. Some cacti can only grow if bats pollinate them. Desert animals would not have enough water without bats.

How Bats Help Humans

Bats eat insects that harm the food humans grow. They also pollinate fruits and vegetables. There would be fewer bananas, avocados, and mangoes without bats.

Scientists are making a new medicine from bat drool. The medicine is called Draculin. It is helping people with heart problems.

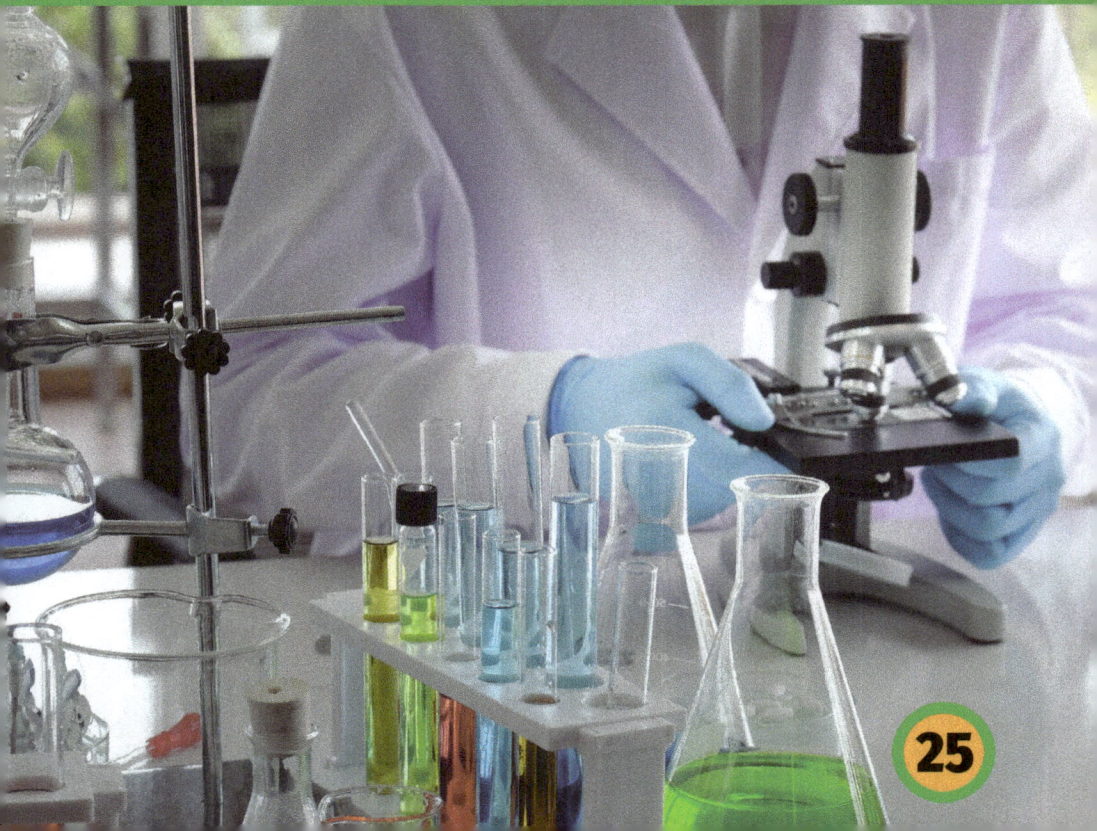

Bats in Danger

Many bats are endangered. This means there are very few of them left. A disease called white-nose syndrome is making bats end their hibernation early. When bats wake up, there is not enough food to eat.

Some bats are hunted by humans. The Mauritian flying fox bat is hunted on Mauritius island. The country sees the bats as pests. These bats are disappearing.

How To Help Bats

Pesticides are chemicals that kill bugs. Bats eat insects that have been sprayed with pesticides. This can make bats very sick. Many people are no longer using pesticides.

Some people do not like bats. They will scare bats away from their homes. Tell your friends and family how helpful bats are. This can help save bats from being forced out of their roosts.

Quiz

Test your knowledge of bats by answering the following questions. The questions are based on what you have read in this book. The answers are listed on the bottom of the next page.

1 What are bat wings made of?

2 What are bat homes called?

3 What are baby bats called?

4 How do most bats sleep?

5 How many kinds of bats are there?

6 What are pesticides?

Explore other books in the Animals That Make a Difference series.

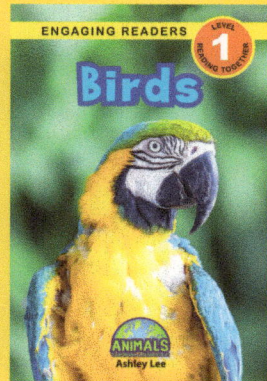

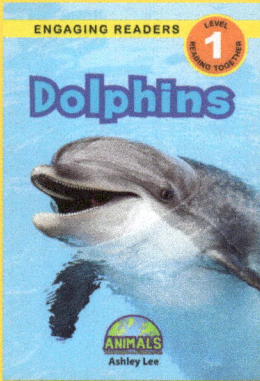

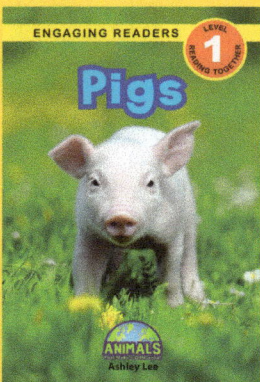

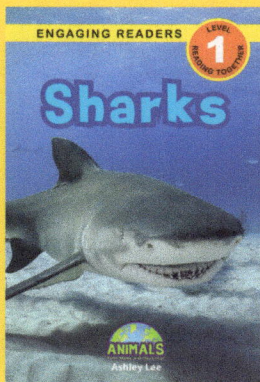

Visit www.engagebooks.com to explore more Engaging Readers.

Answers:
1. Thin skin 2. Roosts 3. Pups 4. Upside down 5. More than 1,300 6. Chemicals that kill bugs

www.ingramcontent.com/pod-product-compliance
Lightning Source LLC
Chambersburg PA
CBHW051234020426
42331CB00016B/3375